Legacy Grandparenting Summit·2023

Table of contents

◇

Only be careful,

and watch yourselves closely

so that you do not forget

the things your eyes have seen

or let them fade from your heart

as long as you live.

Teach them to your children

and to their children after them.

DEUTERONOMY 4:9

◇

Welcome

to the 2023 Legacy Grandparenting Summit!

 You will often hear us express this sentiment: "I want my grandkids in heaven with me!" And wow, are we driven by that desire! Our vision is to infuse the 30-million-plus Christian grandparents in North America with the same passion and then equip them to impact their grandchildren more effectively than ever before for Jesus Christ. This gathering of thousands of Christian grandparents is one more step toward that goal!

Our theme for 2023 is "Light the Way." What a privilege grandparents have to be spiritual lights to their grandchildren, directing them to Jesus. Our amazing lineup of speakers will address our role from various perspectives. And while many of you will be affirmed in what you are already doing with your grandchildren, others will be deeply challenged to take their grandparenting to a level they have not considered before. All of you who attend are going to be blessed, encouraged, and instructed, so don't miss a session! If you do, you will be pleased to know that on the Tuesday after you attend the conference, you will receive a link by email to watch what you missed. You will have through Thanksgiving weekend (November 26) to view what you missed.

Thank you so much for investing your time to listen, learn, and interact. May God use this event to advance His Kingdom in our families. And may many more grandchildren be in heaven with us someday!

Larry Fowler

Larry Fowler
Founder and CEO, Legacy Coalition

Schedule

Times noted in the schedule are for the live site. Host site schedules may vary.

DAY ONE

General Session 1 .... 10am–11:30am
OCBF Worship Team
Larry Fowler
Tony Evans

Break 11:30am–12pm

General Session 2 .... 12pm–1pm
OCBF Worship Team
Jean & Jeremiah Castille

Lunch 1pm–2pm

General Session 3 .... 2pm–3:30pm
Kathy Koch
Mike Singletary

Break 3:30pm–4pm

General Session 4 .... 4pm–5pm
Mark Yarbrough

DAY TWO

General Session 5 .... 9am–10:30am
OCBF Worship Team
Samuel Rodriguez
Mark Gregston

Break 10:30am–11am

General Session 6 .... 11am–12pm
OCBF Worship Team
Crawford Loritts

Lunch 12pm–1pm

General Session 7 .... 1pm–2:15pm
Walt Mueller
Ann Gillies

Break 2:15pm–2:45pm

General Session 8 .... 2:45pm–4pm
Jerry Foster
Hal Habecker
Larry Fowler

*All times are local for all sites except those in the Eastern Time Zone, which are one hour later.

Larry Fowler

Larry Fowler is the founder of the Legacy Coalition. His 50 years plus of ministry leadership, including experience as youth pastor, missionary, and senior executive for Awana, has prepared him for this significant new calling in life. Larry has authored several books on children's and family ministry including *Raising a Modern-Day Joseph,* and his most recent, Overcoming Grandparenting Barriers. In 2012, he was presented with a lifetime achievement award by the International Network of Children's Ministry. Larry and his wife, Diane, live in Riverside, California. They have two children and seven grandchildren.

Join the conversation about this general session on social media by liking and commenting on Legacy Grandparenting Summit posts.

Be sure to include **#grandparentsummit23** in your comment!

INSTAGRAM

FACEBOOK

This is my resolve...

I want my grandchildren in heaven with me,

And I will light the way!

I will be a lighthouse in the middle of a storm,

I will be a porchlight, always welcoming them home.

I will be a north star that can guide their way,

I will be a sunrise, brightening their day.

Because I want my grandchildren in Heaven with me,

I will light the way!

My faith will not fade out,

My desire will not die out, My resolve will not run out.

And my light will not burn out.

My walk will not wimp out,

Until God calls me home.

Because I want my grandkids in heaven with me!

That is my resolve. Is it yours?

Retirement **Reformation**

EMBRACE PURPOSE AND JOY IN YOUR RETIREMENT YEARS

Are you ready to face the potential pitfalls of retirement?
Without a clear purpose, retirement can lead to a sense of emptiness, monotony, and loss of identity. It's about more than just relaxation or grandparenting. At Retirement Reformation, we journey alongside Christ-followers like you, serving as a trusted advisor as you transform your retirement years into a time of **ACTIVE ENGAGEMENT, PERSONAL GROWTH,** and **KINGDOM IMPACT.** We believe retirement is an opportunity to step up and answer God's call in a new and exciting way.

Escape the retirement rut. Embrace the adventure of a purposeful retirement at:

RETIREMENTREFORMATION.ORG

Dr. Tony Evans

Dr. Tony Evans is one of the country's most respected leaders in evangelical circles. As a pastor, teacher, author, and speaker, he serves the body of Christ through his unique ability to communicate complex theological truths through simple, yet profound, illustrations. While addressing the practical issues of today, Dr. Evans is known as a relevant expositor. New and veteran pastors alike regard him as a pastor of pastors and a father in the faith.

Join the conversation about this general session on social media by liking and commenting on Legacy Grandparenting Summit posts.

Be sure to include **#grandparentsummit23** in your comment!

INSTAGRAM

FACEBOOK

God's Love in a Shoebox

It was the first gift he had ever received ...

Vladimir Prokhnevskiy grew up in Ukraine in a family of nine children. Food was a luxury to feed so many mouths; his family survived on rice and potatoes all throughout his childhood. As third from the youngest, Vladimir wore hand-me-down clothes and shared the same pair of tennis shoes between several of his brothers, each taking turns wearing them outside to play. Even a simple toothbrush was a shared necessity between the siblings.

Vladimir and his twin brother

Being very resourceful, his mom made clothes for the whole family. She would wash all the laundry by hand, working so hard scrubbing with a large block of soap that her hands would crack and bleed.

Before the Soviet Union fell in 1991, Vladimir's family experienced heavy persecution for their faith in Jesus Christ. His father was the pastor of an underground church that would meet in the middle of the night either out in the woods or in various apartments. The government was aware of his involvement, and would threaten to send him to Chernobyl to work on the nuclear reactor. Persecution continued even after the fall of communism. The culture taught that belief in God was a sign of weakness.

When Vladimir was nine years old, his family learned about a special Christmas event for low-income families. Together, Vladimir and his siblings made the long journey by riding the bus and then the tram in the middle of a harsh winter. He didn't have warm clothes, but Vladimir was so excited he didn't feel cold at all.

Stepping into the festive outreach event was like transitioning out of a black and white Ukrainian winter into a colorful room of joy and laughter. Welcoming smiles and joyous music filled the space as the Gospel was presented in engaging, child-

Today, Vladimir is motivated to bring the Gospel to the ends of the earth.

friendly ways. And at the very end, Vladimir and his siblings each received their very own Operation Christmas Child shoebox gift. This was the first gift he had ever received.

The bright colors covering each box caught Vladimir's eye. Inside was just as colorful, including a large yo-yo and toy cars, brand-new school supplies and a toothbrush – necessities his family couldn't afford. But his favorite item in the shoebox gift was dental floss. Vladimir thought it was candy because it tasted so minty and good!

Best of all, Vladimir's shoebox gift became to him an example of God's unconditional love. In his culture, bribery was commonplace, so a gift was rarely a gift because something was always expected in return. Most people only ever looked out for themselves, but his shoebox gift gave Vladimir hope that people could be loving and generous. This tangible expression of God's love through an Operation Christmas Child shoebox gift helped him better understand God's free gift of salvation.

In 2000, Vladimir and his family moved to the United States as Christian refugees. Today, Vladimir is motivated to bring the Gospel to the ends of the earth. He loves to pack shoebox gifts together with his wife and sons in order to share God's unconditional love with children all around the world.

Discover more about Vladimir's testimony and the multiplication of believers through Operation Christmas Child in this special episode of Legacy Coalition's weekly webinar, Grand Monday Nights.

LegacyCoalition.com/gmnepisode/gods-love-in-a-shoebox/

Jean & Jeremiah Castille

Jean and Jeremiah Castille are a remarkable Christian couple who have made it their life's mission to spread the Word of God and inspire others. With over three decades of marriage and unshakable faith, they have become well-known figures in the Christian community. Jean is an accomplished author and speaker, while Jeremiah is a former NFL star turned minister. Whether through their books, sermons, or personal encounters, the Castilles are true ambassadors of the gospel and a shining example of what it means to walk in faith.

Join the conversation about this general session on social media by liking and commenting on Legacy Grandparenting Summit posts.

Be sure to include **#grandparentsummit23** in your comment!

INSTAGRAM

FACEBOOK

Perfect for Storytime!

Young children love this new series that teaches a biblical value in each story. Follow along with the cute and curious Otter B as each book ends with a Bible verse and rhyme that reinforces the theme.

CHOOSE YOUR FAVORITE OR GET **ALL 12 STORIES** WHEREVER YOU BUY YOUR BOOKS.

"WE ORDERED THE ENTIRE OTTER B SERIES AND ALL NINE OF MY GRANDCHILDREN **LOVE THEM!**" – SHERRELL

Learning Your Grandchildren's Love Languages (PART 1)

Joannie DeBrito
PH.D., LCSW, LMFT

Just over three decades ago, Gary Chapman wrote a book that was intended to help spouses learn how to love one another well. The 5 Love Languages explains that all of us have a primary and secondary love language that helps us to feel very loved.

If we could discover the love languages of our spouses, we could then show them love in ways that would be most likely to be cherished and appreciated by them. On the other hand, if we assumed that they felt most loved in the ways that we did, we might miss opportunities to love them in ways they found most meaningful.

Additionally, if their love language was used in discipline, it hurts deeper. Love languages are great to use to build up but not to discipline.

Practical tips for learning the love languages of your grandchildren so you can interact with them in a way that helps them feel deeply loved by you.

CONTINUED ON NEXT PAGE

Chapman identified the love languages as:

Words of Affirmation

Quality time

Receiving gifts

Acts of Service

Physical Touch

After the first book, Chapman's concept of the 5 love languages was expanded to include books that discussed how to discover the love languages of children, teens, singles, and coworkers.

In this article, I will offer some practical tips for learning the love languages of your grandchildren so you can interact with them in a way that helps them feel deeply loved by you.

With grandchildren, you have to observe their behavior to get clues about their primary and secondary love languages.

In part one of this article, we'll explore words of affirmation and quality time.

WORDS OF AFFIRMATION

Grandchildren who feel most loved when they hear words of affirmation are those who are more interested in engaging in a conversation with you than playing a game with you.

They are very attuned to what you say. You will see their faces light up if you affirm them, often referring back to a word of encouragement from a previous conversation. This indicates how closely they listened and that what you said made a significant impression on them.

Take the time to talk to these children, using age-appropriate language. Provide unexpected statements of encouragement, either through a conversation or by leaving encouraging notes in their rooms or in their backpacks.

If you have a young grandchild, you will often find that the chatty toddler will develop into one for who words of affirmation is their primary love language. As these grandchildren grow older, take the time to tell them what you appreciate about them at each stage of development. Include those older grandchildren who are emerging into adulthood and those who are having children of their own.

QUALITY TIME

A grandchild who frequently asks you to play with him or her, often wants to show you something, or appears to get upset if you are spending time with another, likely leans toward quality time being his or her primary or secondary love language.

Therefore, when you interact with this child, make sure that you have put all distractions aside (no texting during this precious time!). Provide your full attention and ask what things he or she would like to do with you in the future, making a mental or written note of what activities are favored. Then, plan to do those kinds of activities regularly.

If you live far away from that grandchild but regularly connect via a virtual connection, spend the time online playing a game with each other rather than just chatting.

These grandchildren are also more likely to enjoy gifts that provide opportunities to spend time with you, rather than toys. Consider making up coupons to go for a bike ride, enjoy a picnic in the park together, bake cookies, or camp in the backyard.

Ask teens who feel loved via spending time together to come up with ways that they would like to enjoy quality time with you, and don't forget to make time for those college students and young adults.

If you have had a good relationship with a grandchild who values quality time and you learn that he or she will be coming to visit you or going home for a special holiday, take some time for the two of you to plan some quality time together.

CONCLUSION

Part two of this blog covers the last three love languages: receiving gifts, acts of service, and physical touch. Read Part 2 at:

LegacyCoalition.com/learning-your-grandchildrens-love-languages-part-2/

Be intentional this week, observing and thinking about each of your grandchildren. Have fun discovering their love languages then implement some ways to show them love.

ABOUT THE LEGACY COALITION BLOG

The Legacy Coalition Blog contains hundreds of articles to equip and inspire you to light the way for your grandchildren. Topics include:

• Your grandparenting role and impact

• Overcoming grandparenting challenges

• Practical ideas for connecting with your grandchildren

• Guidance to start or grow a grandparenting ministry in your church

MORE
From the Legacy Coalition Blog:

 (PART 2)
LEARNING YOUR GRANDCHILDREN'S LOVE LANGUAGES

 REASONS WHY ADULT CHILDREN AND GRANDCHILDREN STRAY

 3 WAYS TO BUILD MEMORIES WITH YOUR GRANDKIDS

Find these articles and hundreds more at LegacyCoalition.com/blog

Dr. Kathy Koch

Dr. Kathy Koch (pronounced "cook") is the Founder and President of Celebrate Kids, Inc., based in Fort Worth, TX, and a cofounder of Ignite the Family, based in Alpharetta, GA. She has influenced thousands of parents, teachers, and children in 30 countries through keynote messages, seminars, chapels, and other events. She is proud to be represented by the Ambassador Speakers Bureau of Nashville, TN. She is a featured speaker for the Great Homeschool Conventions, on the faculty of Summit Ministries, and a frequent presenter for Care Net, Axis, and other organizations. She speaks regularly at schools, churches, and pregnancy resource centers.

Join the conversation about this general session on social media by liking and commenting on Legacy Grandparenting Summit posts.

Be sure to include **#grandparentsummit23** in your comment!

INSTAGRAM

FACEBOOK

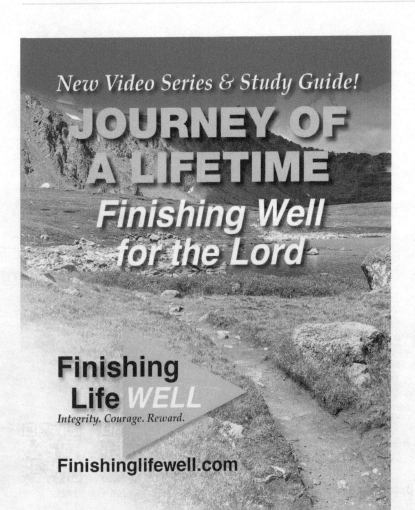

Mike Singletary

Mike Singletary is perhaps most recognized as the Chicago Bears' Middle Linebacker with the ferocious eyes peering across the line into the opposing quarterback's face. He participated in Super Bowl XX where the Bears defeated the New England Patriots and made 10 trips to the Pro Bowl in his 12 years of professional football. He also led the NFL as Defensive Player of the Year three times, and was Bears' team captain for 10 years. Since his retirement from professional football, Mike Singletary has been a regular on the Fortune 500 company lecture circuit. As a motivational speaker, he's known for dynamic talks on leadership, teamwork, and corporate diversity.

Join the conversation about this general session on social media by liking and commenting on Legacy Grandparenting Summit posts.

Be sure to include **#grandparentsummit23** in your comment!

INSTAGRAM   FACEBOOK

GENEROUS KIDS
BOOK CLUB

Grandparenting Matters

A SEMINAR FOR LARGE GROUPS, SMALL GROUPS, AND HOME USE

Your best intro to intentional Christian grandparenting

THREE SEMINAR OPTIONS:

 Live at your church

 DVD or Download

 Live Virtual Event

Host a seminar at your church or in your small group to help grandparents understand and embrace the impact of their biblical role.

This seminar will help you:

- Learn what the Bible says about your influence as a grandparent

- Discover ways to strengthen your relationships with your adult children and positively impact the spiritual development of your grandchildren.

GET STARTED AT
LegacyCoalition.com/seminars

Explore the Legacy Coalition Store

Find all these resources and more at: legacycoalition.com/store

Biblical Grandparenting

Discover culture's misleading messages about grandparenting and gain a clear vision to impact the next generation for Christ.

Equipping Grandparents

Learn how to start a grandparenting ministry in your church so grandparents can reach and disciple the youngest generations.

Discipling Your Grandchildren

Learn engaging and meaningful ways grandparents can disciple their grandchildren and leave a lasting legacy of faith.

Let's Talk Cards

Enjoy these age-specific questions that lead to rich conversations with your grandchildren.

Let's Talk: Holiday Edition

Spark meaningful conversations with your grandchildren at holiday gatherings.

NEW ### Let's Talk: Grown-up Grandchildren

The newest addition to the family of Let's Talk conversation cards, featuring questions that prompt conversations with your grown-up grandchildren.

Promise Cards

Remind your grandchildren about the personal promises of God by including one of these 100 cards with a gift, a note in their lunch, or mailed with a letter.

Long-Distance Grandparenting

Conquer the challenges of nurturing the faith of your grandchildren when you can't be there in person.

Overcoming Grandparenting Barriers

Become equipped to navigate painful family problems with grace and truth.

Raising Your Grandchildren

Explore encouragement and guidance for those parenting their children's children.

Prayers For My Grandchildren Desk Pad / Placemat

Pray the Scriptures daily for your grandchildren. Includes Scripture to pray for many relevant topics

Songs To Inspire Intentional Grandparenting

Nationally-known Christian artists bring original songs to encourage intentional Christian grandparents. Available through bandcamp.com

Grandparenting: Strengthening Your Family and Passing on Your Faith

Grandparenting gives you a biblical foundation for investing spiritually in your grandchildren.

MORE RESOURCES ON NEXT PAGE

LEGACY COALITION STORE CONTINUED

Creation Fun

Create memories and build a godly legacy that will last long after the snacks are eaten, games are played, and crafts are completed.

Celebrate Grandparenting

Celebrate Grandparenting includes 101 activities, in seven categories, and is based on the premise that grandparents and grandchildren celebrate life in many different ways.

Faithful Grandparenting

Grandparents have a unique opportunity to impart knowledge and spiritual wisdom into the lives of their grandchildren-as well as create long-lasting, happy memories.

My Declaration: 8x10 Art Print

By calligrapher Timothy Botts, this powerful declaration expresses your commitment to be an intentional Christian grandparent. Makes a great gift for grandparents in your church. Also available as 12x16 or 18x24 canvas prints, excellent for framing and displaying.

Email info@LegacyCoalition.com for more information.

GrandCoaching™

Guiding Grandchildren With Godly Principles

The Master Life Coach Training Institute offers a 16-part online course to equip grandparents (and parents, too) with the essential tools of Christian life coaching.
This course empowers you to engage your grandchildren in a positive and impactful way, countering the potentially harmful effects of the modern era.

MASTER LIFE COACH TRAINING INSTITUTE
Contact Rodney Love
469-212-3733

Equip your church to love the older generation

2023 exhibitor - Meet Author Isabel Tom

Prepare to Care

a video-based training for adult children & grandchildren

with Isabel Tom
author of
The Value of Wrinkles

valueofwrinkles.com/church

GRAND
Monday
Nights

FREE WEEKLY

Webinar

TO HELP YOU GROW AS A CHRISTIAN GRANDPARENT

Join us Mondays at 7pm Central! With special guest presenters each week, you'll learn how to overcome grandparenting obstacles, build stronger relationships, and nurture your grandchildren's faith.

Recent episodes include:

| How to Stay Drama Free Among Family | Why So Many Youths Are Rejecting Their Childhood Faith – What Grandparents Can Do | The Life-Giving Power of a Grandparent's Blessing |

Legacy
COALITION

Dr. Mark Yarborough

Dr. Mark Yarbrough began his tenure as the 6th president of Dallas Theological Seminary on July 1, 2020. He also serves as Professor of Bible Exposition. Along with his responsibilities of leading DTS, he serves as an elder of Centerpoint Church in Mesquite, TX, and travels extensively leading tours and speaking at conference centers. Mark has authored several books including *How to Read the Bible Like a Seminary Professor*, *Jonah: Beyond the Tale of a Whale*, and *Tidings of Comfort and Joy*. He has been married for over thirty years to Jennifer, his high school sweetheart. They have four adult children, one son-in-law, and reside in Sunnyvale, TX.

Join the conversation about this general session on social media by liking and commenting on Legacy Grandparenting Summit posts.

Be sure to include **#grandparentsummit23** in your comment!

INSTAGRAM

FACEBOOK

Weekend to
Remember.
by FamilyLife

Leave a Legacy for your family by helping them have a great marriage.

FamilyLife's Weekend to Remember is a marriage getaway that has equipped over 1.5 million couples with practical tools & resources. Help your kids and grandkids move toward a oneness that empowers them to leave a godly legacy.

SAVE $100 PER COUPLE
BY USING OUR GROUP NAME:

GPSummit

Scan QR code for a chance to win a
FREE Weekend to Remember registration and other great marriage resources.

Register at WEEKENDTOREMEMBER.COM or call 1-800-358-6329

14 Can't-Overlook Factors (EXCERPT)

Unpacking the GRANDPARENTING acrostic for intentional Christian grandparents.

Larry Fowler
Legacy Coalition Founder

THE GRANDPARENTING ACROSTIC

I've entitled this lesson *14 Can't-Overlook Factors,* Based on an acrostic from *My Declaration* — a declaration I wrote years ago to mark my decision to be an intentional Christian grandparent. I'm going to talk through each letter and unpack one element of Christian grandparenting with each letter.

G—I will Guide Grandkids with Grace

Grace ought to be a characteristic that describes our grandparenting almost more than any other word. In fact, so much so, I think we could rename grandparenting *grace*parenting.

1. What do I mean by grace?

• When you're a parent you obviously have to be concerned with discipline and structure and everything that goes along with parenting. When you get to be a grandparent your perception ought to change and your contribution ought to change. So when you're in the grandparent role it's really important that you think about guiding them with grace. The Bible talks about the grace that we give to other people. and that's really what I'm talking about here.

2. How do we exhibit grace?

- Be quick to say, "I'm sorry."

- Be a question-asker rather than an advice-giver.

- Try to understand, to be gentle

3. Grace is a primary characteristic of grandparenting

R – I will Respect Parent Roles

This is critical, that you as a grandparent respect the role of the parent.

1. While you are still the parent (noun), you no longer parent (verb)

- … unless you're invited to do so. When you try to parent your adult kids then probably it's going to put a barrier up that will inhibit you from being the kind of influencer that you want to be in the lives of your grandkids. That means you need to shut your mouth sometimes when you want to give your opinion about how they discipline, how they keep a schedule, or what their priorities are. You just need to be silent. Silence is a virtue.

- Grandmas, you are not to interfere and give advice unless you're asked how to take care of a new baby or how to handle a toddler. Let them find it out themselves, just like you did. And, grandfathers, the same thing goes for you. Be careful about giving advice to your sons-in-law, making sure that you're not overstepping your bounds and parenting them unless they ask you to do that.

A – I will Abound In My Affection

This one, I think, is the easiest of all to do. This is the one that comes so naturally to us. Here's my take-away for this one that I think is more of a challenge.

1. Loving as God loves us means unconditional

- The challenges really come in as our grandchildren get older. What if they become teenagers and they make some decisions that we don't like? Then we will be challenged regarding our love for them.

- When God loves us unconditionally, it does not mean that he approves of everything you and I do. So, we need to reflect God to our grandchildren in the same way. We are going to love them unconditionally, no matter what they say, no matter what they do. If you and I can't reflect Jesus in this way, who's going to do it in their life?

N – I will Nurture Their Nature

How are our grandkids wired? What are their talents and their abilities?

1. Be observers of our grandchildren

- We will be observers of:
  - → their personality
  - → their gifts
  - → their talents
  - → their inclinations

- Most Bible scholars are agreed that that's probably not the best translation of that verse, that it really means something like this:

CONTINUED ON NEXT PAGE

→ Train up a child according to the tenor of his way, OR...

→ according to his natural bent, OR ...

→ according to his personality, OR ...

→ according to the way he's wired.

- And when we do that, then we will see them not depart from their way.

D—I will Deal With the Dilemma of Distance

If you're going to be intentional and you have grand-kids that live at a distance, you simply have to deal with the distance.

1. Move to be close to the grandkids

- But that's not possible for all of you and, of course, your grandkids or your children don't always "co-operate" (live in the same place).

2. Lean into creativity, consistency, and opportunity

- Creativity—If moving is not an option, you may have to become more creative. If you need some ideas, then Wayne Rice's book Long Distance Grandparenting will be helpful to you because it's full of ideas. (See link at the end of this document)

- Consistency—Don't let your current communication with them wane, just because they're far away. Step up your game. Do what you can to very consistently engage with your grandchildren. Be consistent and you'll watch them come back as years go by.

- Opportunity—Whether that is an opportunity, on a regular basis to communicate by Facetime, video, phone, or some other way, or if it's when you go to see them, make sure that you're taking advantage of that time together.

P—I will Pray With Passion and Purpose

1. Be earnest in prayer

- I have not been the greatest example of someone who is disciplined in their prayer life. I'm a "doer".

- One day I saw James 5:16 in the New Living Translation, and it gave me a lot of hope.

  ... *The earnest prayer of a righteous person has great power and produces wonderful results.*

  The King James Version reads: ... *The effectual fervent prayer of a righteous man availeth much.*

  When I was younger, I didn't know what "effectual" and "fervent" was, and I didn't know "availeth much". When I saw the verse in the New Living Translation, it began to mean so much to me.

- Earnest prayer—It's not how long I pray, it's my mental attitude and the state of mind that is indicated by the word earnest. And I can pray earnestly for my grandchildren on a regular basis, however it fits into how I'm wired.

- Righteous person—James is talking about a practical godliness when he uses the word righteous. It means somebody that is sincerely a Christ-follower, somebody that is pursuing their faith, not perfect, not sinless at all, but sincere in their faith.

- Great power and wonderful results—That's the kind of prayer that we need to be exhibiting as a grandparent. We need to pray with purpose and with passion.

GROUP DISCUSSION QUESTIONS

1. Why does GRACE need to be a key element of intentional Christian grandparenting? How can we tangibly exhibit grace to our grandchildren?

2. Why is it extremely crucial that we step away from our former parenting roles? What can happen if we overstep this?

3. Larry speaks about challenges we face when our grandchildren are older and make decisions we don't like. We are to love them unconditionally, because if we don't, who will? Why is this important? Can you share a personal story of experiencing this?

4. How are you narrowing the gap and keeping a solid relationship with your grandchildren who live at a distance?

5. What are some tips to share with your group about praying for your grandchildren?

_____

_____

_____

_____

The lesson excerpt that begins on page 42 is taken from *Equipping Intentional Grandparents*, a small group study series that consists of a workbook and free accompanying videos.

You can access the video and Part 2 of this lesson, along with five more 2-part lessons and videos for Equipping Intentional Grandparents, by registering at LegacyCoalition.com/eig

SMALL GROUP

Studies for Christian Grandparents

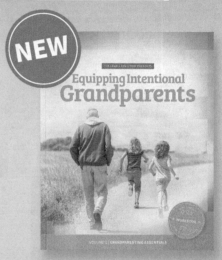

NEW

"This study made me realize how important grandparenting is. It opened the door for my husband and I to take wonderful trip with our grandkids. We feel much closer to them now."

—JUDY, SAN DIEGO, CA

Get started at:

Legacycoalition.com/eig

Legacy
COALITION

Samuel Rodriguez

Samuel Rodriguez, lead pastor of New Season, one of America's most influential megachurches according to Newsmax, is the president of the National Hispanic Christian Leadership Conference. Rodriguez stands recognized by CNN, FOX News, Univision, and Telemundo as America's most influential Latino/Hispanic faith leader. The Wall St. Journal named him one of the top 12 Latino leaders and he was the only faith leader on that list. Rodriguez is the recipient of the Martin Luther King Jr. Leadership Award and has advised Presidents Bush, Obama, and Trump. He also frequently consults with members of Congress to advance life, religious liberty, and biblical justice initiatives including immigration and criminal justice reform. He is the best-selling author of *Be Light* and executive producer of three films including *Breakthrough*.

Join the conversation about this general session on social media by liking and commenting on Legacy Grandparenting Summit posts.

Be sure to include **#grandparentsummit23** in your comment!

INSTAGRAM

FACEBOOK

LEGACY Grand parenting Podcast

Listen in on fascinating discussions about navigating today's world as a Christian grandparent. Hosted by Wayne Rice and John Coulombe with a variety of special guests.

Recent episodes include:

Confessions of an Unintentional Grandparent	Helping Your Grandchildren Enjoy the Bible	Helping Your Grandkids Manage Their Digital Screens
FEATURING KEN DAVIS	FEATURING KEITH FERRIN	FEATURING WALT MUELLER

Listen anytime via Spotify, Pandora, Amazon, Apple Podcasts or at LegacyCoalition.com/podcast

Legacy
COALITION

Mark Gregston

Mark Gregston is an author, speaker, radio host, and the founder of a residential counseling center for struggling teens located in Longview, Texas. Mark's passion for helping teens can be seen in his 50 years of involvement with families as a youth pastor, Young Life area director, and now, as the Executive Director of Heartlight, a residential counseling center where he has lived with and helped over 3,000 teens. Mark has been married to his high school sweetheart, Jan, for 48 years, and has 2 kids and 4 grandkids. He lives in Longview, Texas with the staff at Heartlight, 60 high school kids, 25 horses, and a prized donkey named Toy.

Join the conversation about this general session on social media by liking and commenting on Legacy Grandparenting Summit posts.

Be sure to include **#grandparentsummit23** in your comment!

INSTAGRAM

FACEBOOK

Bible Stories with Beautiful Art

This collection contains 250 beloved Bible stories from both Old and New Testaments. Each spread includes classic art paired with a Bible story right from Scripture. Perfect for storytime or bedtime.

978-0-8254-4646-7
$27.99

This keepsake volume combines actual Scripture with stunning, high-quality traditional artwork to bring the timeless Christmas story to life. Also includes ideas for celebrating the season.

978-0-8254-4832-4
$17.99

Dr. Crawford Loritts

Dr. Crawford Loritts is founder and president of Beyond Our Generation, a ministry committed to encouraging and helping shape the next generation of Christian leaders. For 15 years, he served as senior pastor of Fellowship Bible Church in Roswell, Georgia, and has authored nine books including *Your Marriage Today... and Tomorrow*. He travels the world as a featured speaker and is the host of two radio programs, Living a Legacy and Legacy Moments. He serves on the boards of several ministries including Cru, FamilyLife and Chick-fil-A. He and his wife Karen have four grown children and eleven grandchildren.

Join the conversation about this general session on social media by liking and commenting on Legacy Grandparenting Summit posts.

Be sure to include **#grandparentsummit23** in your comment!

INSTAGRAM

FACEBOOK

Next Step

Looking to take another step toward becoming a more intentional Christian grandparent?

We recommend:

Equipping Intentional Grandparents

A small-group study series with free accompanying video content.

Dr. Walt Mueller

Dr. Walt Mueller is the founder and President of the Center for Parent/Youth Understanding and has been working with young people and families for over 40 years. As a result of his work with CPYU, Walt has become an internationally-recognized speaker and author on contemporary youth culture. He has written extensively on youth culture and family issues and is the author of dozens of books: *The Space Between: A Parent's Guide to Teenage Development* (Zondervan); *Opie Doesn't Live Here Anymore: Where Faith, Family, and Culture Collide* (Standard Publishing); *Youth Culture 101* (Zondervan); *Engaging The Soul of Youth Culture: Bridging Teen Worldviews To Christian Truth* (InterVarsity Press); and the critically acclaimed Gold Medallion Award winner, *Understanding Today's Youth Culture* (Tyndale House). A graduate of Geneva College (B.A.) and Gordon-Conwell Theological Seminary (M.Div.), Walt earned his doctorate at Gordon-Conwell in "Ministry to Postmodern Generations."

Join the conversation about this general session on social media by liking and commenting on Legacy Grandparenting Summit posts.

Be sure to include **#grandparentsummit23** in your comment!

INSTAGRAM

FACEBOOK

CHRISTIAN GRANDPARENTING NETWORK

*Equipping grandparents
to represent Christ
to the Next Generation*

- GrandCamp
- GrandDay Out (one-day camp)
- Prayer Tools
- Grandparent@Prayer Groups
- Conferences and Retreats
- Scripture Cards
- Books, blogs and other resources

ChristianGrandparenting.com

CHRISTIAN
GRANDPARENTING
NETWORK

TRANSFORM A LIFE WITH LOVE

Become a Wrap-Around Grandparent Today

Imagine channeling your lifetime of wisdom, experience, and love into a cause that can change lives. The Retirement Reformation's "Legacy of Love: The Wrap-Around Grandparents Initiative" invites compassionate seniors like you to step into the role of a grandparent for children in foster care.

Get involved today at
go.retirementreformation.org/legacy2023

RR RETIREMENT
REFORMATION

LEGACY
OF LOVE
The Wrap-Around Grandparents Initiative

Dr. Ann Gillies

Dr. Gillies is trained jointly in psychology and theology and retired from private practice after 25 years of clinical counselling focused primarily on individuals struggling with complex traumatic stress as a result of chronic childhood sexual abuse. She is an ordained pastor, international speaker, author, and founder of Restoring the Mosaic, a ministry that seeks to educate and inform politicians, community leaders, and pastors across Canada to restore the mosaic of our God-given identity: individually and nationally. She's authored a number of books with more on the way.

Join the conversation about this general session on social media by liking and commenting on Legacy Grandparenting Summit posts.

Be sure to include **#grandparentsummit23** in your comment!

INSTAGRAM

FACEBOOK

A number of years ago, a grandparent asked Legacy Coalition founder, Larry Fowler, why he started Legacy Coalition. He answered:

"I want my grandchildren in heaven with me..."

Through the Legacy Coalition, Christian grandparents are awakened to...

The Higher Bar
Many thousands of Christian grandparents are becoming aware of **the higher standard** that Scripture gives them for their role.

Cultural Giants
Never before has a generation experienced **cultural giants** like our grandchildren face—the negative aspects of social media are devastating the faith of too many of them. As grandparents awaken, they are wielding their powerful influence to counter this tool of Satan.

The Urgency
Psalm 90:12 tells us "**numbering our days" leads to wisdom.** That speaks of awareness about how short life is, how brief our opportunities are to influence. We believe we must act NOW.

The need...

We are praying for 200 new monthly donors from those who participate in the Legacy Grandparenting Summit.

Will you be an answer to that prayer?

Your financial partnership will help more Christian grandparents impact the desire of their hearts—that their grandchildren will be in heaven with them!

"...and I know there are millions of Christian grandparents who want the same!"

Become a monthly donor today at
LegacyCoalition.com/donate

Legacy
COALITION

Jerry Foster

Jerry is from Des Moines, Iowa and has been married to Nancy for 45 years. They have four children and 15 grandchildren. They also have been foster parents for numerous children throughout the years. Jerry and Nancy were speakers at FamilyLife's "Weekend to Remember" marriage conferences for 22 years and Jerry had been a speaker at various international conferences on leadership. He is the author of *LifeFocus, Achieving a Life of Purpose and Influence*. Jerry is the founder of Foster Group, a financial planning and wealth management company.

Join the conversation about this general session on social media by liking and commenting on Legacy Grandparenting Summit posts.

Be sure to include **#grandparentsummit23** in your comment!

INSTAGRAM

FACEBOOK

Hal Habecker

Hal and his wife, Vicki, live in Plano, Texas. They have three children and six grandchildren. Hal has served for 43 years in three different Dallas-based ministries: First Baptist Church, Dallas, The Christian Medical & Dental Associations, and Dallas Bible Church. In 2015, he launched Finishing Well Ministries, encouraging and mobilizing retiring boomers and a senior generation for the kingdom of Christ. He is a graduate of Taylor University ('71), and Dallas Seminary (ThM.'78) and Denver Seminary (DMin.'88). Connect with Hal at finishingwellministries.org.

Join the conversation about this general session on social media by liking and commenting on Legacy Grandparenting Summit posts.

Be sure to include **#grandparentsummit23** in your comment!

INSTAGRAM

FACEBOOK

Thank you to our sponsors!

 Retirement **Reformation**

 **BARNABAS** FOUNDATION

 FamilyLife®
A Cru Ministry

 PRAY for ME CAMPAIGN

 the value of wrinkles

 CELEBRATEKIDS

 MASTER LIFE COACH TRAINING INSTITUTE

 CHRISTIAN GRANDPARENTING NETWORK

 Finishing Life WELL
Integrity. Courage. Reward.

 BRAVE BOOKS

 Engage to Go Ministries

 Christian Community CREDIT UNION

Made in the USA
Las Vegas, NV
07 October 2023

78719283R00044